To

Danny

From

Cousins Amanda & Megan

To Anjali and Makarand Mhasane, for making life beautiful!
R.M.

Written and compiled by Mary Joslin
Illustrations copyright © 2014 Ruchi Mhasane
This edition copyright © 2014 Lion Hudson

Published by Lion Children's Books
an imprint of
Lion Hudson plc
Wilkinson House, Jordan Hill Road,
Oxford OX2 8DR, England
www.lionhudson.com/lionchildrens

ISBN 978 0 7459 6404 1

First edition 2014

Acknowledgments
All unattributed prayers are by Mary Joslin and Lois Rock, copyright © Lion Hudson.
Prayers by Sophie Piper and Elena Pasquali are copyright © Lion Hudson.
Bible extracts are taken or adapted from the Good News Bible © 1994 published by the Bible Societies/HarperCollins Publishers Ltd UK, Good News Bible© American Bible Society 1966, 1971, 1976, 1992. Used with permission.

A catalogue record for this book is available from the British Library

Printed and bound in China, November 2013, LH17

Bible Promises
for a Little Boy

Written and compiled by Mary Joslin
Illustrated by Ruchi Mhasane

LION
CHILDREN'S

God loves you

"God loves you, so don't let anything worry you or frighten you."

<small>DANIEL 10:19</small>

God has counted each sparrow that twitters,
God has counted each leaf on the tree,
God has counted the children on earth:
I know God has counted me.

God hears your prayers

Jesus said, "When you pray, go to your room, close the door, and pray to your Father, who is unseen. And your Father, who sees what you do in private, will reward you."

MATTHEW 6:6

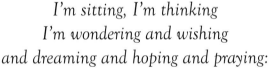

*I'm sitting, I'm thinking
I'm wondering and wishing
and dreaming and hoping and praying:*

*I'm asking, I'm seeking,
I'm truly believing
that God will hear all that I'm saying.*

God guides you

God promises to be near you always, to teach you. If you
wander off the road to the right or the left, you will hear
his voice behind you saying, "Here is the road. Follow it."

From Isaiah 30:20–21

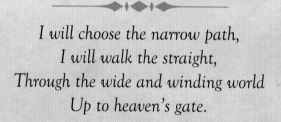

I will choose the narrow path,
I will walk the straight,
Through the wide and winding world
Up to heaven's gate.

Sophie Piper

God gives you wisdom

If you pray for wisdom, God will give it to you.

The wisdom from above is pure first of all. It is also peaceful, gentle, and friendly; it is full of compassion and produces a harvest of good deeds.

FROM JAMES 1:5, 3:17

May all my deeds
be wheat
not weeds.

God blesses your good deeds

God says this: "If you put an end to every injustice and unkindness; if you help those who are hungry or in need, then the darkness around you will turn to the brightness of noon. I will always guide you and satisfy you with good things."

FROM ISAIAH 58:9–11

*A little seed
unfolds its leaves
and grows up to the light;
and I will lift
my face to heaven
and learn to do what's right.*

God provides all you need

Don't be all upset about what you will eat and drink. Instead, be concerned with his kingdom, and he will provide you with these things.

<small>FROM LUKE 12:29, 31</small>

God feeds the birds that sing from the treetops;
God feeds the birds that wade by the sea;
God feeds the birds that dart through the meadows;
So will God take care of me?

God clothes the flowers that bloom on the hillside;
God clothes the blossom that hangs from the tree;
As God cares so much for the birds and the flowers
I know God will take care of me.

SOPHIE PIPER

God will shepherd you

God says this: "I myself will be the shepherd of my sheep, and I will find them a place to rest.

"I will look for those that are lost, bring back those that wander off, bandage those that are hurt, and heal those that are sick."

EZEKIEL 34:15, 16

Dear God, you are my shepherd,
You give me all I need,
You take me where the grass grows green
And I can safely feed.

You take me where the water
Is quiet and cool and clear;
And there I rest and know I'm safe
For you are always near.

BASED ON PSALM 23

God will forgive you

Jesus said, "Do not judge others, and God will not judge you; do not condemn others, and God will not condemn you; forgive others, and God will forgive you."

<small>Luke 6:37</small>

From the mud
a pure white flower

From the storm
a clear blue sky

As we pardon
one another

God forgives us
from on high.

<small>Sophie Piper</small>

God comforts you

Don't worry about anything, but in all your prayers ask God for what you need, always asking him with a thankful heart. And God's peace, which is far beyond human understanding, will keep your hearts and minds safe in union with Christ Jesus.

PHILIPPIANS 4:6–7

I sit still and quietly
in this, my quiet place,
and think of good and lovely things
and God's unfailing grace.

ELENA PASQUALI

God strengthens you

Those who trust in the Lord for help will find
their strength renewed.
They will rise on wings like eagles;
they will run and not get weary;
they will walk and not grow weak.

Isaiah 40:31

Holy Spirit, come
like the winds that blow:
take away my fear;
help my courage grow.

Holy Spirit, come
like a flame of gold:
warm my soul within;
make me strong and bold.

God leads you onwards

Do not cling to events of the past
Or dwell on what happened long ago.
Watch for the new thing I am going to do:
I will make a road through the wilderness.

Isaiah 43:18, 19

Father, lead us through this day
As we travel on our way.
Be our courage, be our friend,
Bring us to our journey's end.

God protects you always

The Lord will protect you from all danger;
he will keep you safe.
He will protect you as you come and go
now and for ever.

PSALM 121:7–8

May I lie down and sleep in peace
secure in God's great love.
Though cradled on the rock of Earth
I'll dream of heaven above.

Jesus said, "Let the children come to me, and do not stop them, because the kingdom of God belongs to such as these."

MARK 10:14